J FOY Child Coll 19058

Fox

The King's falcon.

Date Due			
OCT 4 72			
Apr. 16 73			

CURRICULUM CENTER
J. EUGENE SMITH LIBRARY
EASTERN CONN. STATE COLLEGE
WILLIMANTIC, CONN. 06226
Library
Frederick R. Noble School
Willimantic, Connecticut

DEMCO

THE KING'S FALCON

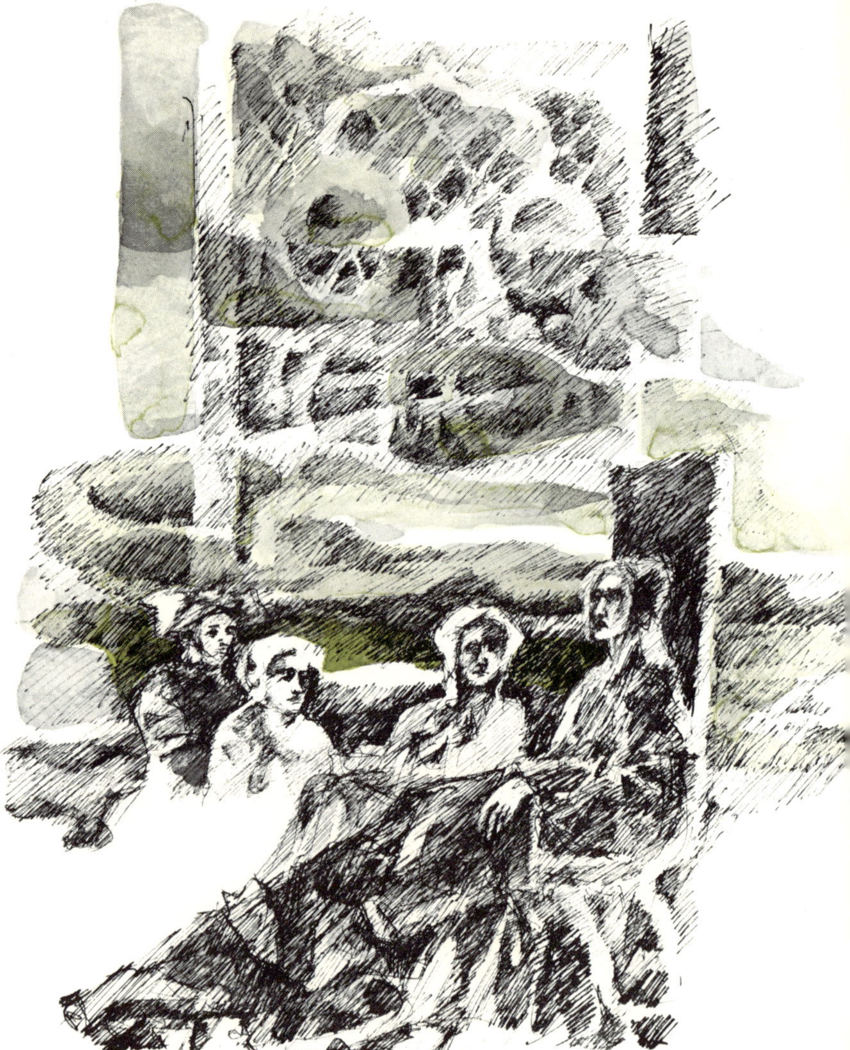

THE KING'S FALCON

by Paula Fox
Illustrated by Eros Keith

BRADBURY PRESS
Englewood Cliffs, New Jersey

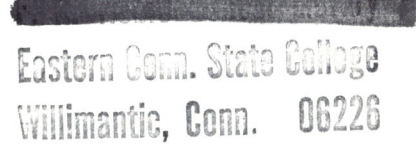

Copyright © 1969 by Paula Fox
Copyright © 1969 by Eros Keith
All rights reserved. No part of this book may be reproduced in any form or by any means, except for the inclusion of brief quotations in a review, without permission in writing from the publisher. Library of Congress Catalog Card Number: 69-13322. Manufactured in the United States of America
First printing

The text of this book is set in 14 point Caslon Old Face. The illustrations are two-color wash and ink drawings, reproduced as halftones.

To James Purdy

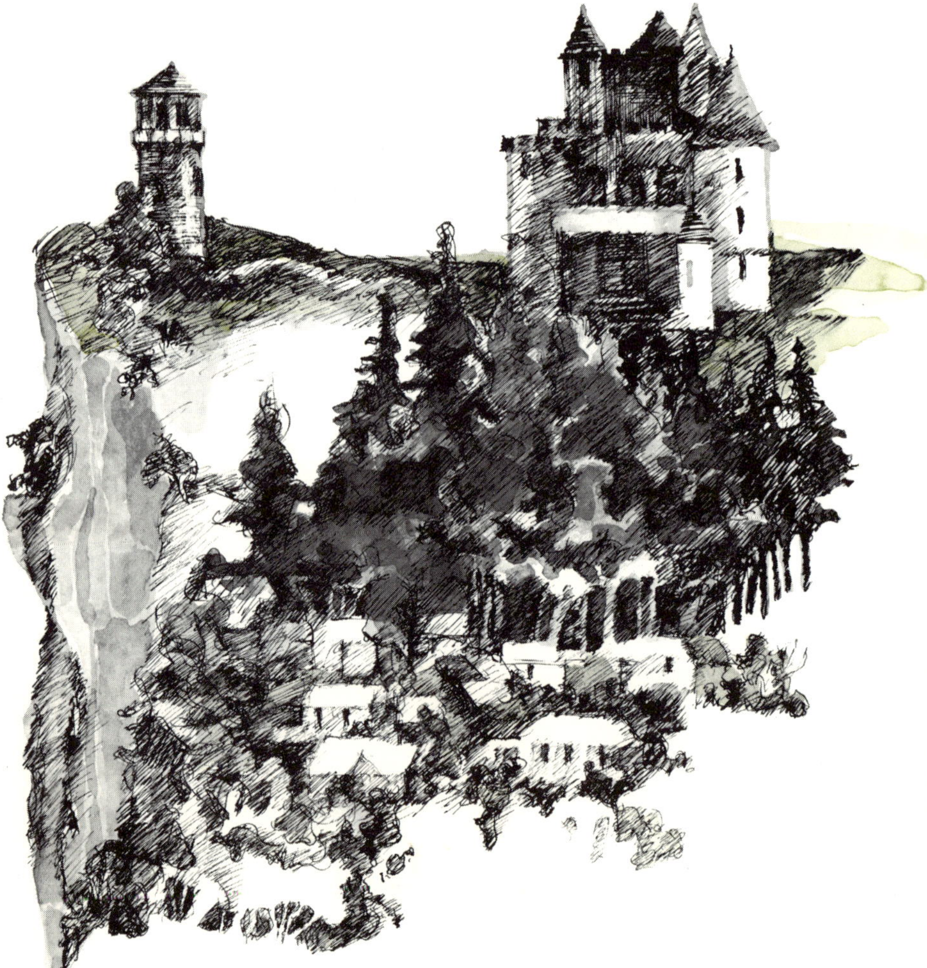

A TOWER STOOD WHERE A CLIFF ROSE TO ITS HIGHEST POINT OVER THE SEA. FROM IT, THE LAND SLOPED down to a narrow valley. There was a village at its southern end and a castle at the northern end. A small but thick forest grew between the village and the castle, and on either side of the forest were meadows of grass all bent northward because of the prevailing wind that arose every afternoon during the milder seasons and blew through the valley.

"My kingdom waves like a banner," said King Philip. His wife, Queen Gertrude, replied, "I doubt it."

These foolish words had the effect of making the King feel foolish.

There were kings, Philip knew, who rode their chargers for many days before they came to the borders of their domains. Philip had no charger. There was only one horse in his kingdom, a mean-tempered, red-eyed old devil who belonged to the peasant in the village who grew cabbages. As for riding for many days to the borders of his domain, Philip could see it all from the castle rampart—the forest, the meadows, the village and the tower, and beyond all, the sea which belonged, as far as the King knew, to no one.

The castle itself was old and small, damp and dark. The tower was squat and moss grew in the cracks between the rough-hewn stones out of which it had been built. The dozen or so cottages in the village were so close to the ground and so humble in appearance that from the castle they looked like carelessly heaped stones.

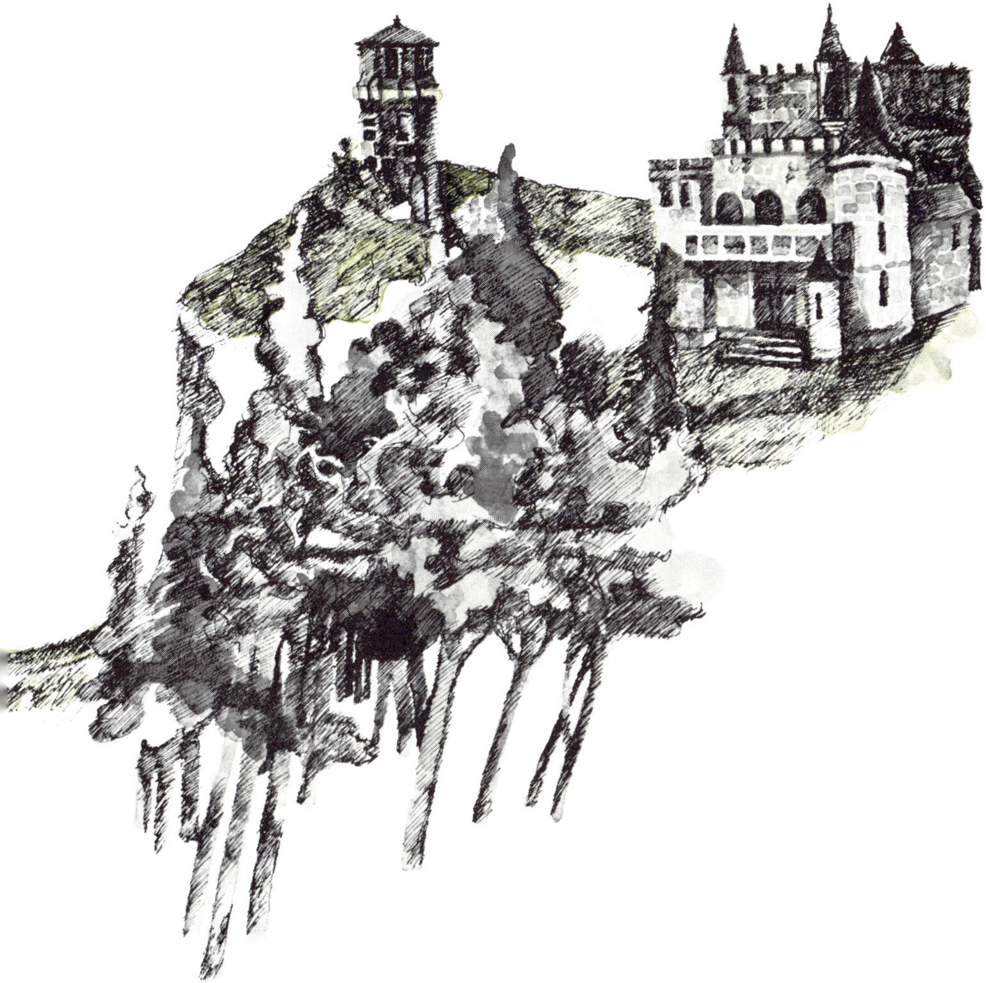

The peasants paid little attention to the King unless the Queen was by his side. Then they doffed their caps and stared respectfully at the ground. The King was not offended by their behavior, as he had no interest in ruling over anyone.

On Sundays, when the peasants did not work, they often passed the time quarreling. When they came to the castle to complain about each other to the King, Philip was never able to decide who was to blame.

But the Queen had no such difficulty. "It's his fault," she would say, pointing to one of them.

"But we haven't heard his side of the argument," the King would protest. "Never mind," the Queen would say. "An argument has no sides."

Gertrude was much older than Philip. At the time their marriage was arranged, their two countries had been at war for forty-three years.

The war was a miserable affair which was neither won nor lost by either side. The populations became so reduced that there were only a few old men left alive. There was no one for **Gertrude to marry.**

Then the kings grew bored with the war and between them devised a story that Gertrude and Philip had been smitten with each other as a result of an exchange of letters between them.

Since Philip was five years old at the time, and Gertrude was already twenty-seven, and since it was known that neither of them could read or write, no one believed this fabrication. But everyone pretended it was true since it brought peace.

They were married when Philip was fifteen. The wedding celebration was very meager because neither kingdom had even enough potatoes left in its dungeons to make a good soup.

"I married beneath myself," the Queen once said to one of the three cousins who served as her ladies-in-waiting.

"But there is no one higher than a king," the cousin had exclaimed.

"I doubt it," said the Queen.

In his own mind, the King divided the year not into months and weeks but into two parts, Possible and Impossible. Possible included the late spring, summer and early fall. Impossible meant the seven months of winter. If he had only been a bear he could have covered himself with leaves and slept through that awful time. It was then that the whole court, as well as the pigs, chickens and dogs, sheltered together in the main hall of the castle, huddling around the huge fire that burned in the center of the room. There was no chimney to funnel away the smoke which, especially on damp days, was so thick it was hard to tell whether one was sitting next to a pig or a dog. Everyone's eyes stung. Everyone coughed day and night. The Queen wore all her robes at once and made the three cousins sit around her to keep off the drafts.

The flagstone floor was covered with mud,

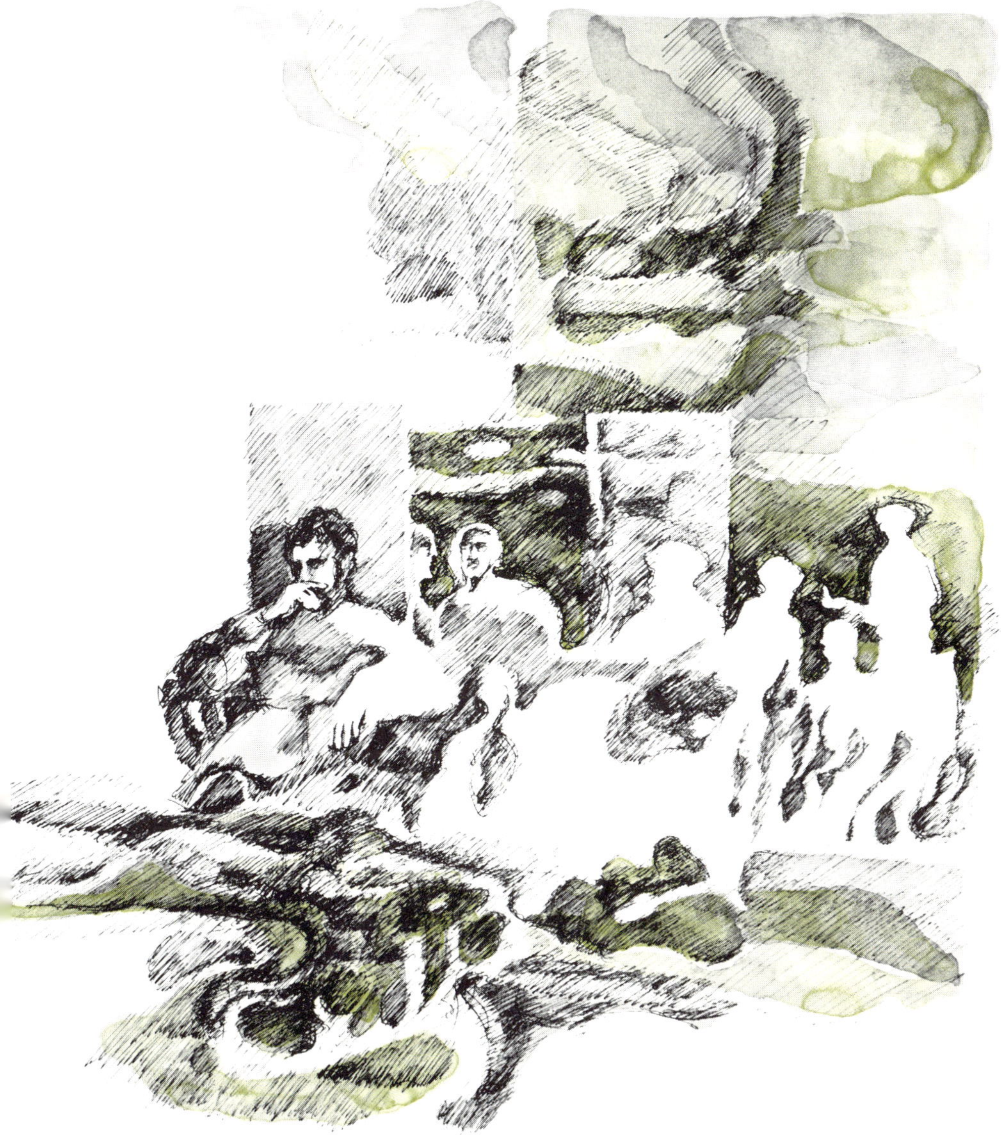

and in places where the flag was uneven there were little frozen lakes like fragments of glass. Nearly everyone gossiped and chattered in the winter mornings: the two young pages, the King's three attendants, the cook, the court musician, the master of the hounds, the kingdom's only Baron, a friar, and whatever visitor was staying on for a few months. But during the long, bitterly cold afternoons, nearly everyone fell into a sullen silence, broken only by the disheartened clucking of a hungry chicken, or the trickle of water running down the walls from the melting snow or the damp creak of wet logs shifting in the fire.

Although the King could not read, he had an extraordinary memory and could recall everything he had ever heard at his father's court years before. Unhappily, these memories only increased his desolation, for the stories which had so excited his imagination when he had heard them as a child concerned the great adventures of the old times, the brilliant histories of knights long dead, the forgotten crossroads of far countries where traveling fairs had once lighted up the nights and enlivened the days.

He had been born too late. Everything had passed him by. What was there to look forward to in the melancholy squalor in which he lived?

He stared into the flames of the fire, his head bursting with memories of other people's memories. But then he thought of the falcon. Standing up so abruptly that his chair crashed to the floor, the King walked to a far corner of the hall.

In this corner, no pig or dog or chicken was allowed. It seemed to the King that here the air was sweet, the walls less damp, the floor clean.

Here the hooded falcon sat on her perch. The falconer lay on his straw bed beside the perch. When the King approached, the falconer arose.

"Unhood her," the King said softly.

The falconer carefully removed the leather cap which fitted over the falcon's head. It was so quiet in the great hall that the King heard the scrape of wood on stone as someone near the fire righted the chair he had overturned.

The King inclined his head forward ever so slightly as if he were bowing to the falcon.

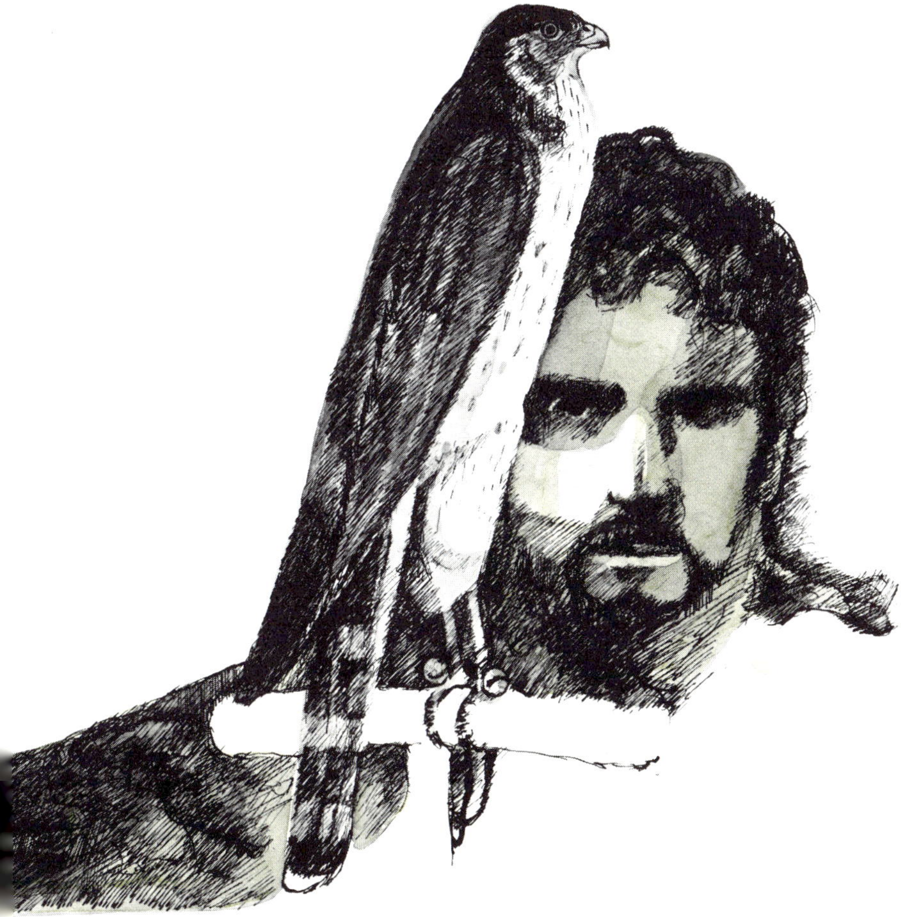

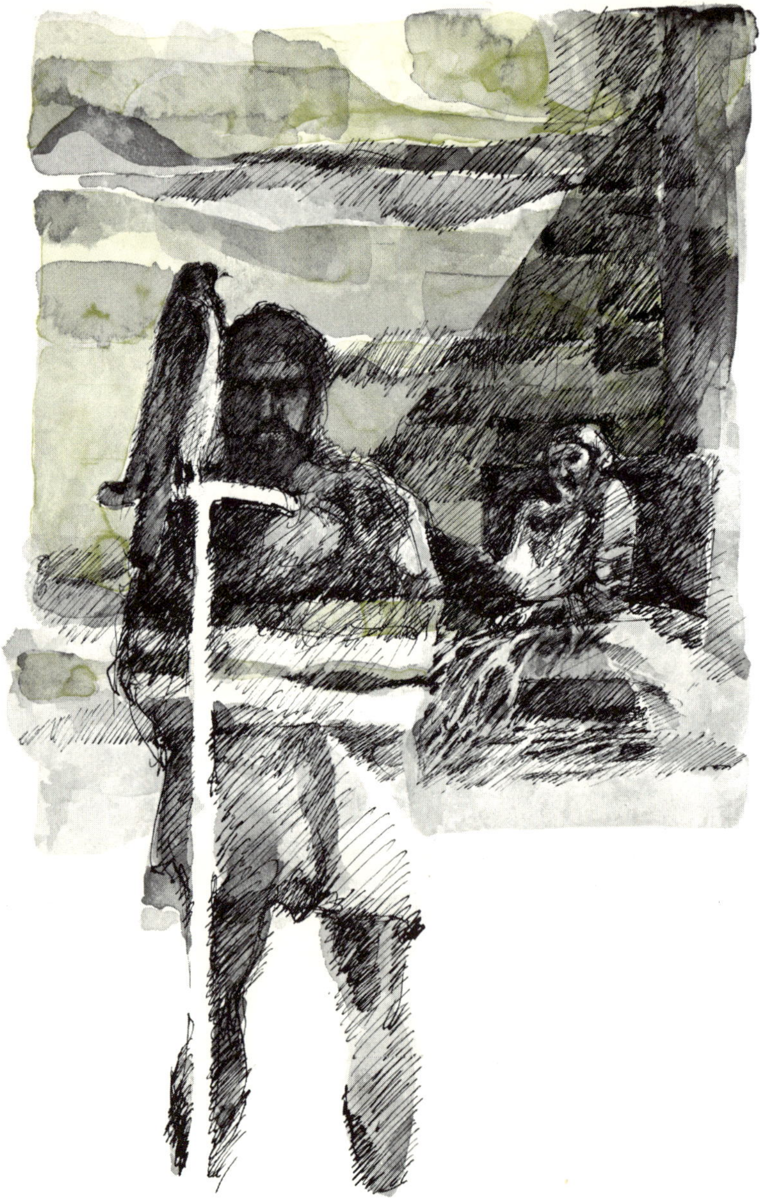

THE FALCON SAT LIKE A STATUE OF A BIRD ON THE BASE OF HER OWN THICK LEGS, HER LONG TALONS curled around the perch. Her hind toes, small unsheathed daggers, stuck straight out behind her. There were leather straps around her legs and a metal bell tied to each foot.

The falconer watched the King impassively. He knew the King might stand there for as long as an hour staring at the falcon. He did not know what the King was thinking, and he did not especially care. But he felt the force of the King's thoughts which, in the falcon's presence, rose like of flock of starlings. At such moments the falconer saw that the King and the falcon in their silent watchfulness resembled each other.

The falconer had been born in the village but had left it in his youth. He had learned the art of falconry at a court far from King Philip's small patch of a kingdom. Then, one day, he had returned with this same falcon on his fist. She had been an eyas then and her flight feathers had not yet replaced the down which covered her. The falconer had trained her, teaching her to come to the lure, always under the King's intense observation.

"Why does she always come back to you?" the King had once asked him as the falcon rose in great ever-widening circles until she had reached that pinnacle of flight the falconer called her point of pride.

"She returns to me by reason of her own will," the falconer said.

"Ah . . ." the King had sighed.

The falcon suddenly moved her head. The brown and white feathering of her face, the dark feathering around her large luminous eyes, were like the shadows which coursed across the land on a brownish cloudy day. The falconer shifted his weight slightly from one foot to the other. Sometimes he grew weary of the King's absorption in the bird. But he didn't complain. He was content as long as there was a place for him and the falcon.

Only once had he requested anything. He had asked the King for a horse. After the falcon had made her kill, it was often hard for him to get to her quickly enough to stop her from gorging herself on it. A horse would have made his life more easy.

But the King said he had no money to buy a horse. The Queen had sent for a tapestry wall-hanging from Gobelin which had depleted the treasury entirely. It was pointless to tax the peasants who had nothing except their small plots of land, by virtue of which they had in any case to supply the court with produce. The kingdom was so poor that the King hadn't a single piece of armor, and the court subsisted on cabbages most of the winter.

"Hood her," the King said. The falconer obeyed and his hands were so expert, the falcon seemed unaware that she had been slipped from day into night. The King went back to his seat by the smoky fire and looked deeply into the flames.

When the King was not thinking about the glorious times he had been born too late to enjoy, he asked himself questions. Why are animals not given speech such as ours? Why does the water on the strand below the tower rise and fall at set intervals? Why are people born kings or peasants or falconers?

There were a hundred more questions, but

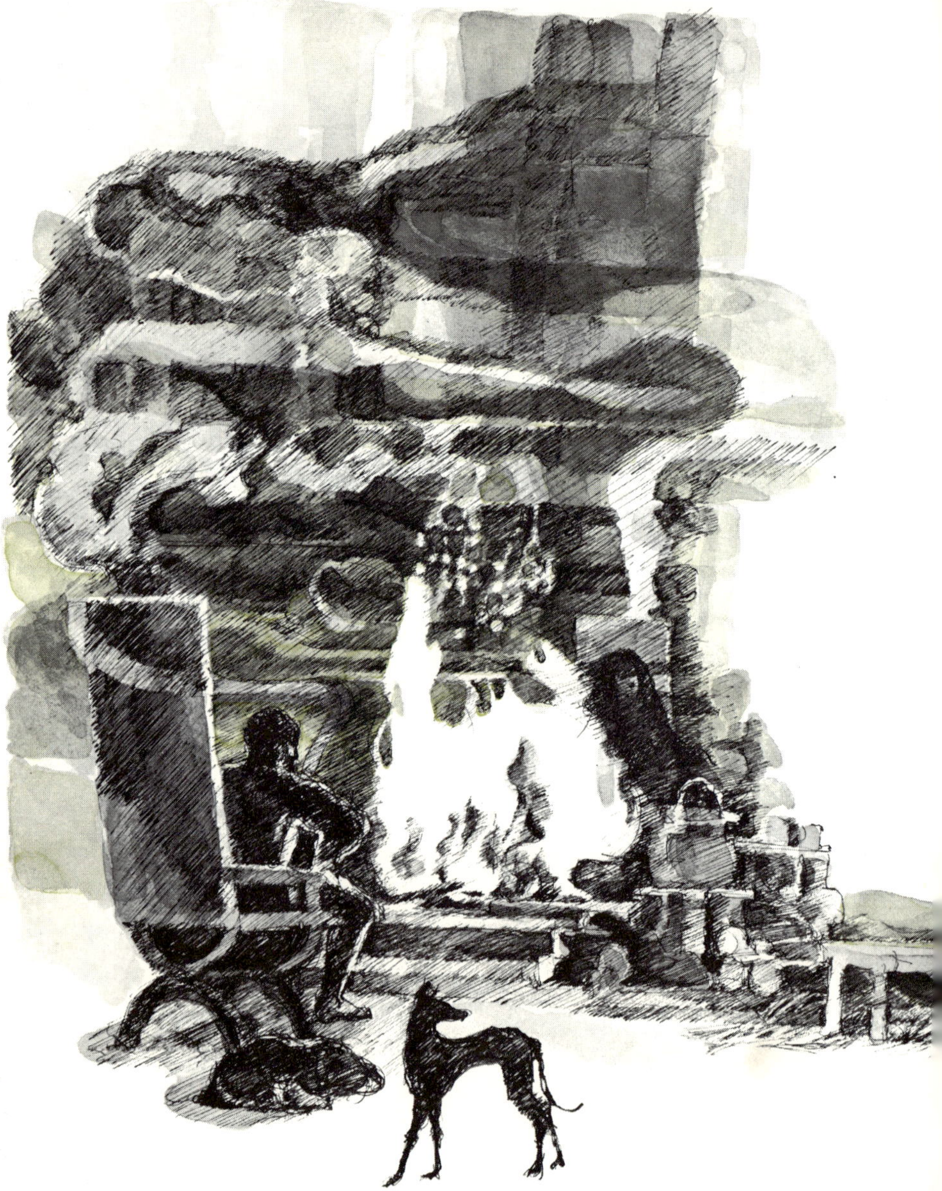

the one to which he came back most often was the riddle of individual fate. Why couldn't he have been born a falconer himself?

How was it that he had not had to learn anything to be a king? The falconer, the son of a peasant, had learned falconry. Even the court musician, a silly grinning fellow, had learned to play the flute. "But I can do nothing," Philip told himself. Why, he did not even know how cabbages grew!

At that moment, the Queen pushed aside one of the cousins and peered at the King through the smoke.

"What are you thinking about?" she asked crossly.

"Nothing," he replied.

"I doubt it," she said.

A great clamor rose suddenly from outside the castle gates.

"Aha!" exclaimed the Queen animatedly. The King sighed and braced himself for the usual babble of accusation. The Queen rose and commanded that the massive wooden doors be opened. As they swung back, several peasants rushed into the hall and, still brandishing their fists at each other, sank to their knees.

The King glanced over at the falconer, who appeared to be sleeping. The bird was motionless. "How beautiful she is," the King whispered to himself, and his heart lifted. One of the villagers saw the King's elated expression and imagined that a decision favorable to him had been reached even before he had pleaded his case.

"Thank you, thank you, My Lord," he cried, knocking his forehead against the flagstone.

"Take him out and behead him!" muttered the King under his breath.

"Don't be silly," said the Queen who had overheard him. Then she turned to the kneeling peasants. "Come!" she said. "Inform us of your latest quarrels, scandals and disagreements. But make sure they are amusing!"

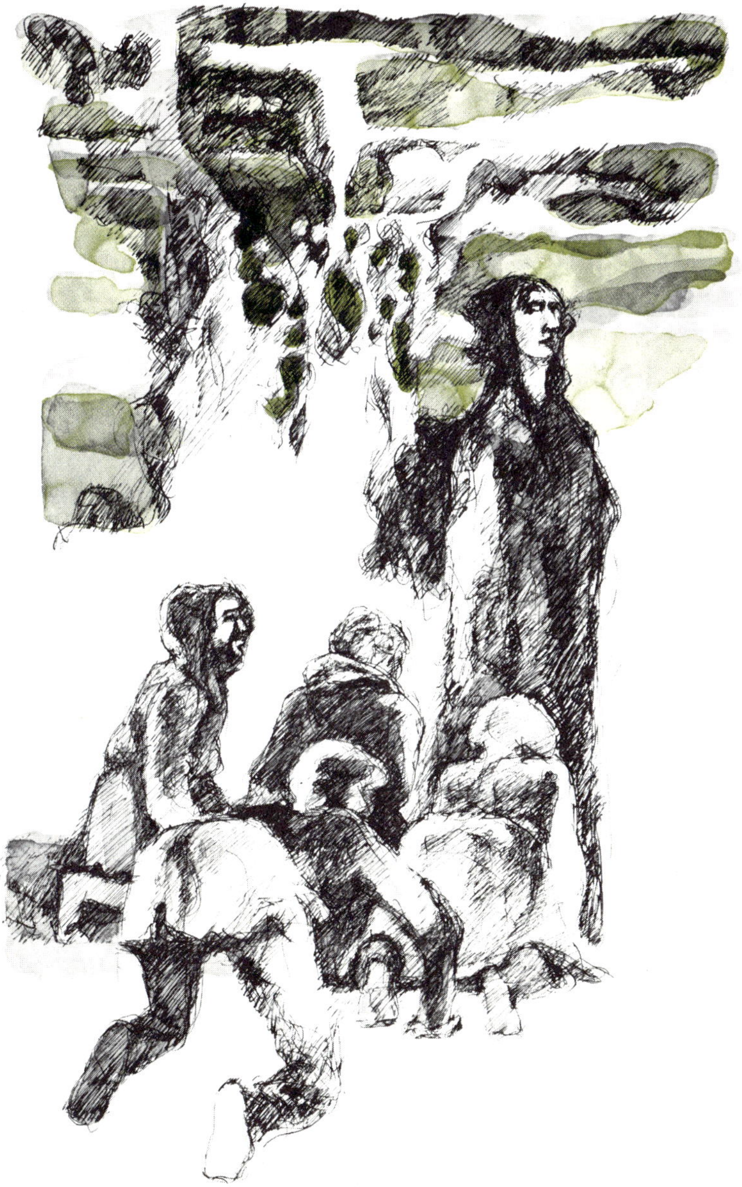

On a warm morning in May, the King and the Falconer walked on the path which led to the tower. The hooded falcon was perched on the falconer's gauntlet.

Most of the court was deployed about the meadow near the castle. Even the old Baron lent his services to the task of fastening a vast net to posts in the ground. The Queen and the cousins watched the proceedings from beneath the branches of a great red-leafed tree. The Queen's eyes glistened. She was anticipating the moment when flocks of small birds would come to feed on the gooseberries which grew so plentifully there. When the birds had sated themselves, the net would be drawn over them and, struggling feebly, they would be taken off to the cook who would make them into pies, saving the feathers for the Queen to sew on her gowns.

The King despised such sport. He thought it ignoble, based as it was on the deception of the hidden net.

F. R. Noble School Library
Eastern Conn. State College
Willimantic, Conn.   06226

They neared the tower. From below the cliff, the King heard the watery mumble of the sea as the waves washed over the pebble-strewn shore.

The falconer began to climb the narrow stone steps in the tower, the King a few steps behind him. Was it he who carried the bird, the King wondered, or was it the bird who carried the falconer in her curved talons?

They reached the very top where a few planks made a kind of platform. The King breathed deeply of the dank air, which smelled of the roots of plants. He would have liked to have lived in the tower. If he had been able to spend even a few days alone in such sweet privacy, a thousand new questions would occur to him.

The falcon's feathers shone in the sunlight which poured through the openings between the blocks of stones. The King looked out over the countryside, then at the sea. The falconer narrowed his eyes to see better. His face, gray and lined and old, was thoughtful.

"Look!" he said suddenly to the King, forgetting his manners. Since they were out of earshot of the Queen, Philip didn't bother to reprove the old man. With his glance he followed the direction of the falconer's gesture. At first, he saw nothing but the sheer drop of the cliff. Then, gradually, he was able to make out an object caught between the crooked limbs of a scrawny tree. It was an eyrie.

"A nest," he said.

"A falcon's nest," said the falconer firmly.

The King pressed up against the damp stones and leaned out to see better.

"There are two eyases in it," said the falconer. At that moment they both saw the male hawk, the tiercel, circling not far from the nest. In his talons he held what appeared to be a pigeon. Then the falcon flew out from her nest. The tiercel relinquished the pigeon, and as it fell the falcon caught it and returned to her young.

The falconer looked steadily at the King but said nothing. It seemed to Philip that he could perceive clearly in the falconer's eyes what was in his own mind.

"Between the two of us," the falconer began somewhat hesitantly, "we could capture one of them." He was silent then, and his expression was not that of a man who is uncertain of the truth of what he has said, but rather of the appropriateness of saying it at all.

"Yes," the King said at last. "But no one must know of it. Only the two of us." He fell silent, astonished at his own words.

After their return to the castle, the falconer went about gathering up what they would need, and he was so quiet, so unobtrusive that no one questioned him. The King observed the falconer's preparations from a distance, trying to behave in his customary way.

But if Gertrude was not clever, she was quick enough to sense any difference in the atmosphere. She followed him about, questioning him closely as to his thoughts. When she had no success with that, she insisted on telling him long boring stories about the peasants which he had heard a hundred times.

Finally, exasperated beyond endurance, she cried, "There's something in your mind which you are hiding from me!"

"I was wondering why animals do not have human speech," the King replied mildly. "And why the sea rises and falls on the shore. And why some people are born kings or peasants and others falconers."

"Shocking!" cried the Queen. But she looked contented in her triumphant way. "Anyone knows the answers to such stupid questions."

She looked around to see that the Baron and the friar and the three cousins were attending to her words. "Animals do not speak, the sea rises and falls, and people are born kings and queens because that is the way things are supposed to be."

The three cousins giggled and applauded daintily. The Queen then made for the kitchen to see what the cook was doing with the birds caught that morning in the net.

Walking with his deliberate step, the falconer

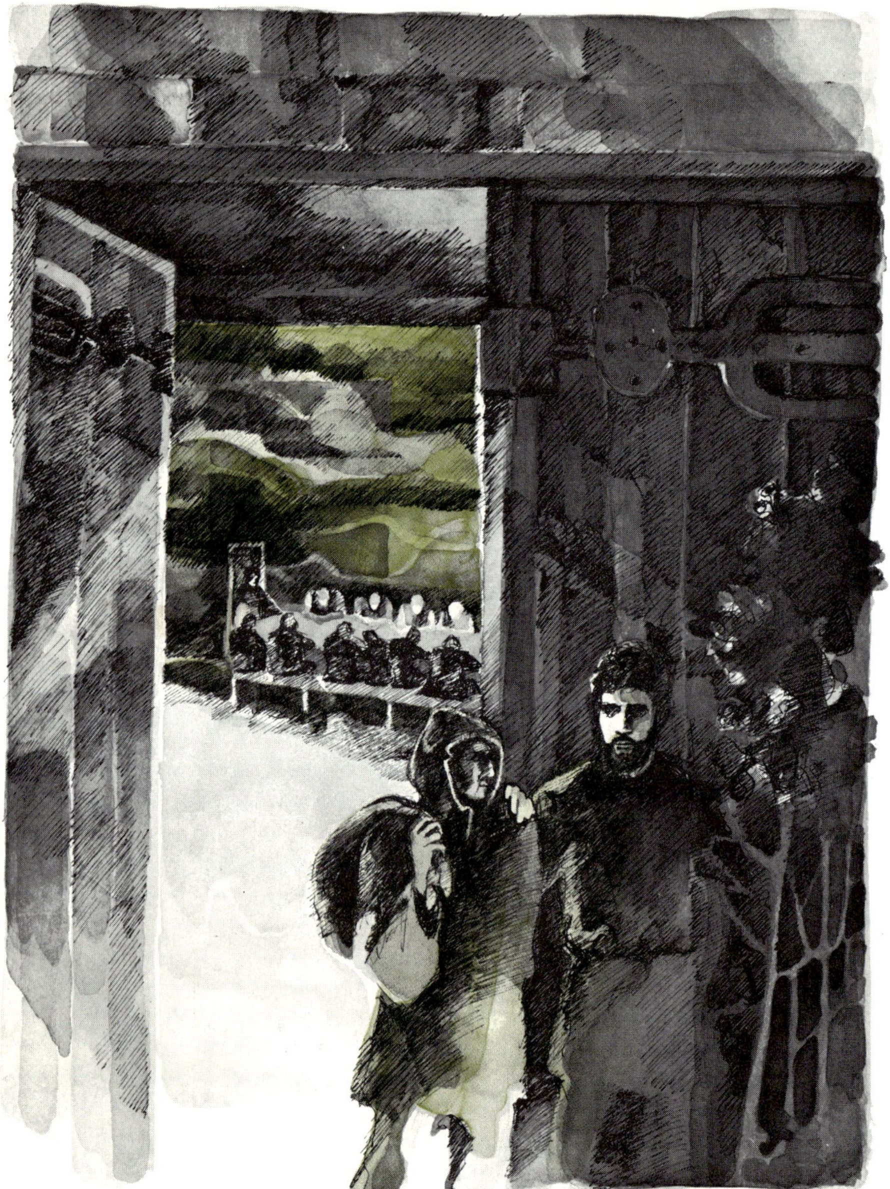

passed the King. "I have everything we will need," he said in a low voice, without looking up.

The King's heart seemed to fly up to his throat and for a moment he could not speak because of excitement.

"Good!" he managed to say at last. "After the meal."

The Queen came back to the great hall. "I will have a new robe made entirely of dazzling feathers," she announced.

"Then," said the King to himself, "you will look like a dazzling chicken."

The delicate twilight of May gave an amber cast to the long table, the massive benches, the two roughly carved royal chairs, even to the Queen's drab skirts where they touched the dusty stone floor. Stupefied by the bird pasties they had consumed, the puddings and the heavy wine, most of the court drowsed over their empty plates. But the King and the falconer had eaten lightly, and now both rose from their seats as though a single shared thought had decided their actions. The falconer went to his corner and from beneath the straw of his bed pulled out a sack.

He joined the King who was waiting just beyond the castle door. They stood silently for a moment. The sky was turning the dark purple-blue of early evening. A faint breeze ruffled the grass of the meadow. The falconer looked up at the castle. The King knew the falconer was distressed because he had had to leave the falcon behind on her perch.

"Perhaps," Philip said softly, "it will not take us long."

The falconer said nothing. There was no special expression on his face. The King thought, he too is hooded, like his falcon. He touched the old man lightly on his shoulder, and they began to move toward the tower.

At the edge of the cliff the falconer knelt and peered down. Then he turned to the King.

"We must tie the rope around the tower. There is nothing else here that will hold my weight," he said, kicking at a small twisted tree that grew near his foot.

"Will there be enough rope?" asked the King.

"I am not sure," replied the falconer.

From his sack, the falconer took the rope, ran it around the tower, tied it and then brought the other end around his own waist.

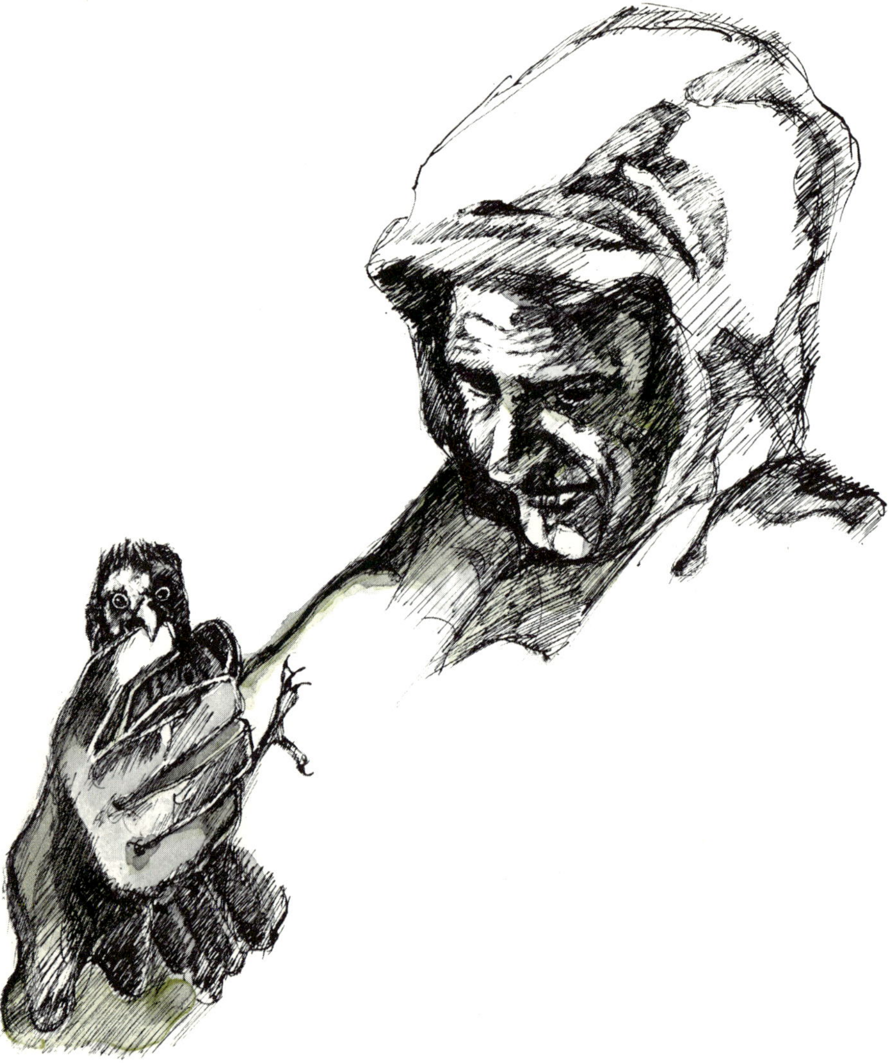

"You must let it out slowly," he said.

The King was pleased by the falconer's tone, which held none of the artifice of court speech.

When the moment came to lower the falconer, the King felt afraid, as though he were casting the old man into the sea. The last thing he saw was the falconer's gloved hands, thick and dark like tree roots clinging to the rope.

Slowly, he let out the coiled lengths. "Enough!" came a loud whisper from somewhere in the darkness below. The breeze cooled the King's face, damp from his exertion. Then there was an explosion of sound, the screeches of angered, frightened birds.

"Bring me back," came the falconer's urgent voice.

The King hauled on the rope. Slowly, the falconer came into sight, one hand on the rope, his ascent marked by the sound of his boots as they struck against the face of the cliff. Finally he was standing next to the King. He lifted the thumb of one glove. By the faint light from the early stars, the King made out the huge beak, the shining eyes and the white down of a young hawk which bit and clawed against the confining hand that held her.

THE SUMMER UNWOUND LIKE A SKEIN OF THE BRIGHT THREADS WHICH THE THREE COUSINS USED for embroidering birds and leaves and flowers on squares of cloth. It was the best time of the year. The iron weather was forgotten. Pigs, chickens and dogs no longer filled the main hall with their animal complaints. The Baron napped in the hot savory sunlight of the meadow. The peasants, calmed by the promise of adequate harvest, rarely quarreled. Sweet air filled the castle like a cascade of mountain water and cleansed the walls of the acrid smell of smoke.

But the King was too busy to think about the weather. Day after day he made his way to the tower where he and the falconer were training the young falcon.

Her white down had been replaced by long flight feathers. She had learned to perch on the King's gauntleted hand and hardly ever fell off to hang helplessly by her jesses, the leather straps attached to her legs. The King, because

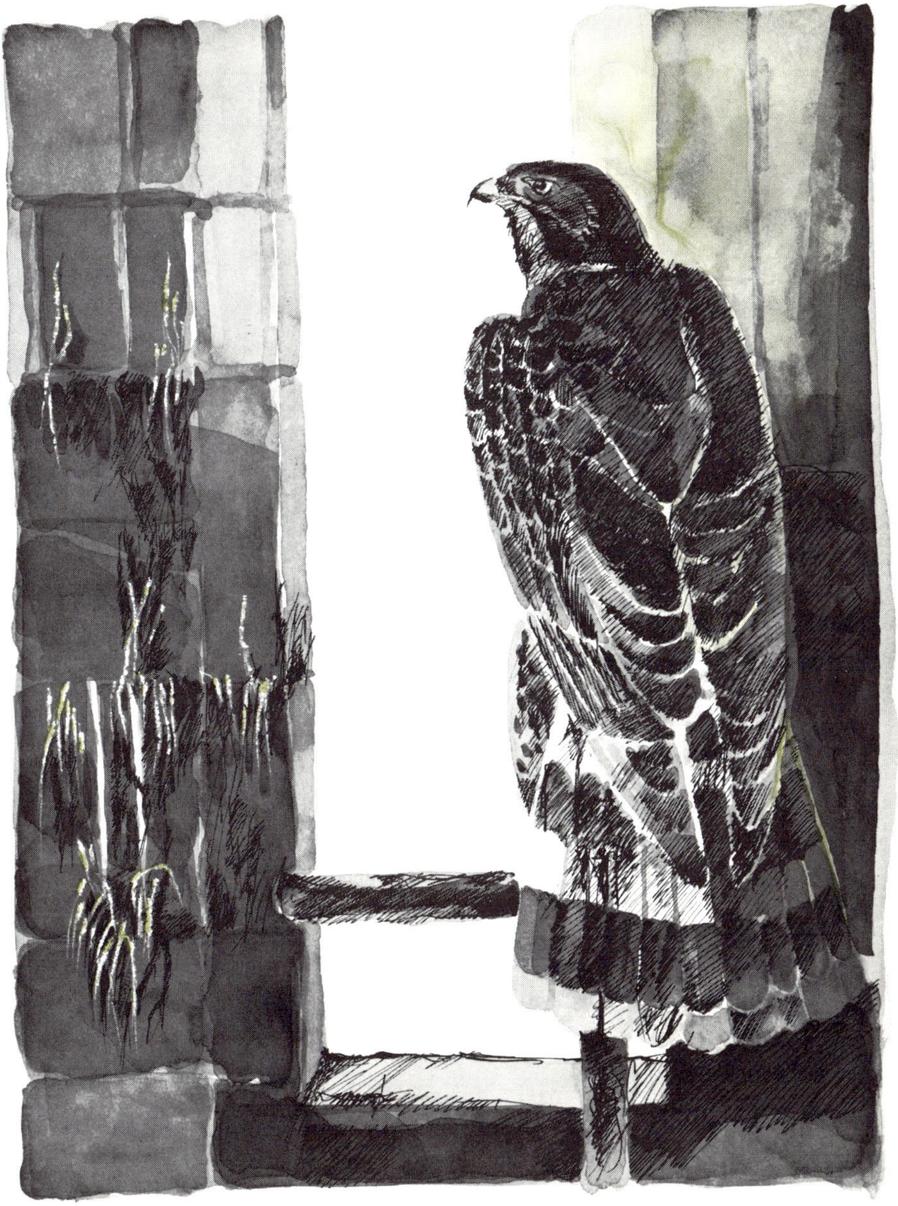

of his long observation of the falconer, was soon able to hood the falcon without distressing her. The falconer presented him with a lure which he had made himself. Next to the falcon, this square of leather ornamented with feathers seemed to the King the most beautiful thing in his kingdom.

"When she has learned to strike it as though it were a flying bird, she will be able to fly free," the falconer said.

The thought of that first free flight alarmed the King. "What if she doesn't return?" he asked.

"Sometimes they don't," said the falconer.

"And if she doesn't," the King said to himself, "has there ever been such a happy time in my life as this summer? What will I have lost?" But still, he was worried.

One morning the falconer said, "Today."

"Today?" repeated the King.

The falconer nodded. "Perhaps we should wait a little longer?" suggested the King hopefully. The falconer looked grave and shook his head.

On that day, the Queen was cross because the sky was gray. She feared it would rain. She had set her heart on a picnic in the meadow and, as was usual when she felt thwarted, she took to following the King about, harassing him with idle questions.

"You can hardly expect me to change the weather!" he cried at last, after she had asked him what he was hiding from her for the sixtieth time.

She stared at him silently for a long moment. Then she said, "You know something I don't know."

He was struck by her words. Never before had she attributed to him a knowledge greater than her own. "It is possible," he said sternly. She turned on her heel and set off toward the three cousins who were sitting in a clump in a corner of the hall.

The falconer waited for him at the tower. The old falcon was hooded and sitting on a perch in the sunlight. The King's falcon sat on the falconer's wrist. Just inside the tower entrance, the King saw a live lark lying on the stone floor, its feet tied together.

"I will cast the falcon up," the falconer said. He removed the long strip of leather that connected the jesses to his hand. "At first, she will expect to be pulled back. Then she will discover she is free. She will rise. If she is hungry enough, if we have trained her well, if she is not more clever than we think, she will strike the lark when I release it. Then we will go and fetch her when she comes to ground."

The King could not speak. He wanted to hide in the tower.

"Now!" said the falconer, and he threw his arm up, the falcon clinging to it. Then he waved his arm in small circles, and the falcon flew from it. For a second, she seemed to hover there, just above them. All at once, she drew, in her flight, a great low circle, then went higher and higher until the King thought she had flown straight into the sky.

The falconer released the lark, which shot from his hands like an arrrow. As the King looked up, he saw the falcon at the pinnacle of the circles she had made in the air, circles which seemed to form a huge bell. Suddenly she dropped in a swoop so swift the King could only just keep her in view. She hit the lark. In an instant there was a shower of feathers which drifted slowly to the earth.

"Done!" said the falconer.

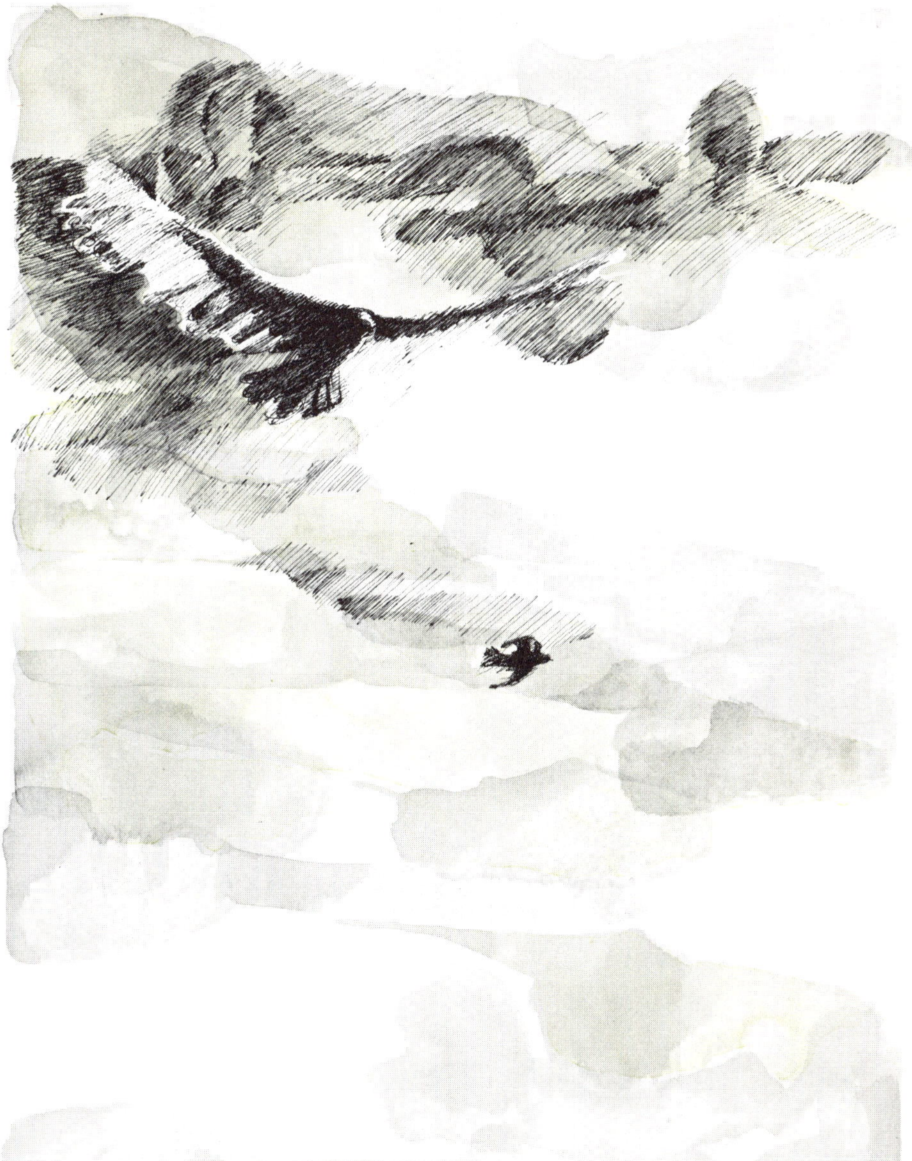

They found her not far from the tower in a clump of grass. She was tearing at the dead lark.

"We will let her have it all," said the falconer. "Next time she will remember what she was given and return to you again."

When they got back to the tower, the falconer said to the King, "You will make a good falconer."

The King was exultant.

But then, thinking of what he must do next, he grew pensive. He did not know when he had begun to think of leaving his kingdom. Perhaps it was at that moment when the falconer had lifted his thumb and revealed the young falcon in his hand. Now it seemed as if the idea had always been in his mind, waiting for an occasion to be spoken aloud.

"I have something secret to say to you," the King said.

The falconer waited.

"I do not want to be King."

To the King's relief, the falconer did not appear to be astonished.

"I intend to depart as soon as I can," the King said.

"What will you do?" asked the falconer.

"Why, I will be a falconer," replied the King.

"How will you eat?"

"There must be other kingdoms where a good falconer will be welcome," said the King.

"I am sure of that," said the falconer. For the first time, the King saw the falconer smile.

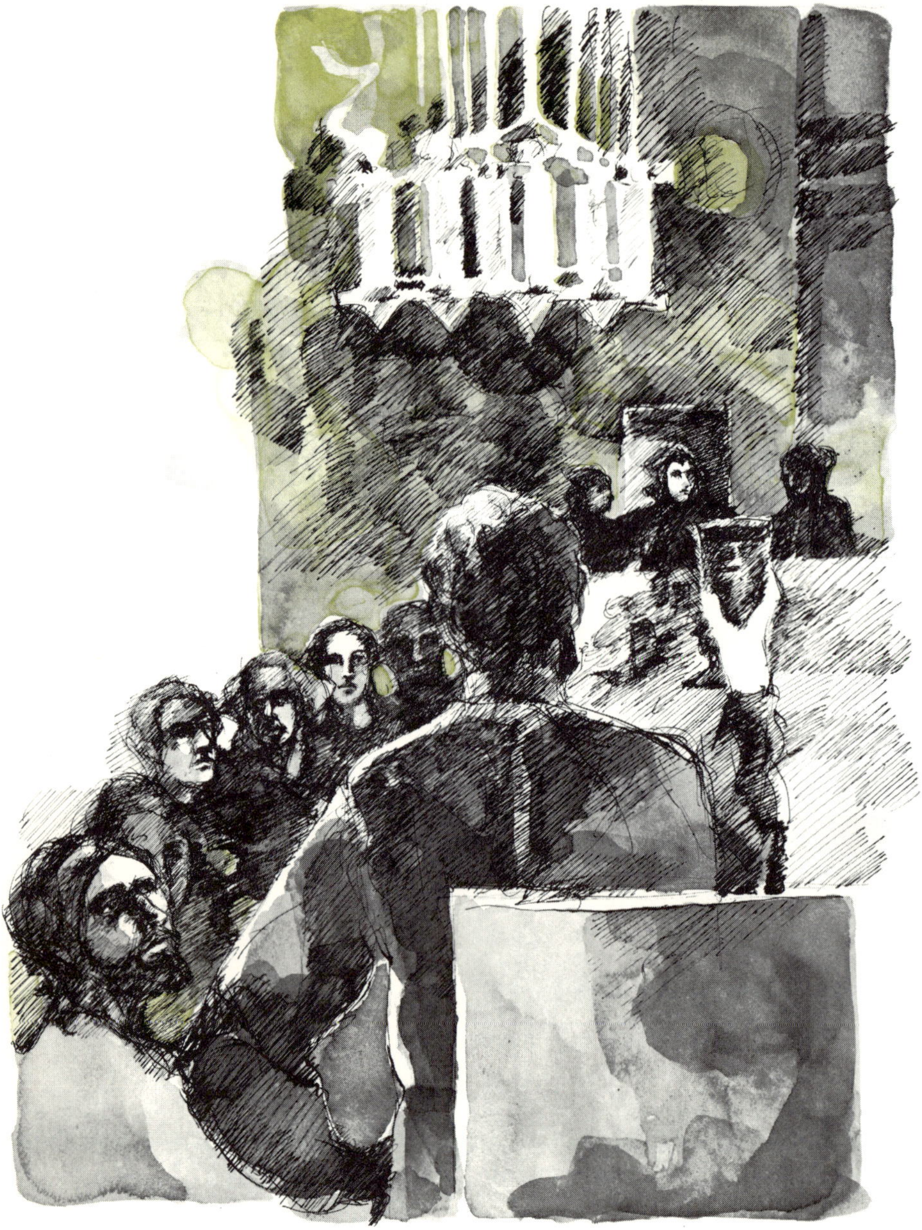

EACH NIGHT FOR A WEEK, THE KING HID A LOAF OF BREAD IN THE FALCONER'S SACK. HE STOLE, FROM HIS OWN kitchen, a wheel of sour cheese which he disliked so much he knew it would last him a long time. Then he added a goatskin of wine and three onions. He had no need for other clothes. His own were so shabby that no one would think him royal.

After he had filled the sack with provisions, he spent long hours in the tower, looking out over the countryside. It would take no more than one hour to escape the castle, go through the meadows, the woods and the village. Once he had left the village, he would be in another kingdom, although whose land it was that bordered his own, he did not know.

The summer was coming to an end. Cricket voices filled the long light-filled evenings. One night the King insisted that everyone remain at the long table. He called for more wine. He demanded that everyone, even the pages, drink to the toasts he proposed to make. The Queen, surprised by such uncharacteristic kingly behavior, did not even argue.

"To the summer!" cried the King, and as everyone lifted their cups, he shouted:

"To the gooseberries!"

"To the tapestries!"

"To the tower!"

"To the cook!"

"To me!" the Queen interrupted.

"To you!" Philip said, then he continued, "To the castle! To the Baron! To the peasants! To the kingdom's noble steed! To the three cousins!"

And by the time the King proposed the very last toast, "To the King's falcon!" everyone except himself and the falconer had fallen asleep.

Philip arose at once. The falconer ran silently to his corner where he took from beneath the straw the sack of provisions. They both tiptoed to the doors and swung them open. The night outside was dark and fragrant and there was a very faint chill in the soft air.

The King took from his finger his only adornment, a ring which had been placed on it years ago by someone in his father's court. He breathed deeply, joyously.

"Take it," he said to the falconer. "If you must leave this place after I've gone, you can exchange this jewel for gold, not much, I'm sure, but enough to keep you for a while."

"What shall I tell them?" asked the falconer, looking back at the castle.

"Tell them a falcon flew off with me," the King said.

"Be careful when you go through the village," the falconer warned him. "There'll be a great hue and cry if you're seen."

"I will move like a shadow," said the King.

He and the falconer went to the tower to get Philip's falcon. Once she was perched on his fist, Philip set off down the slope. The falconer returned to the castle. Neither of them turned to look back. In any case, it would have been too dark for them to have seen each other.

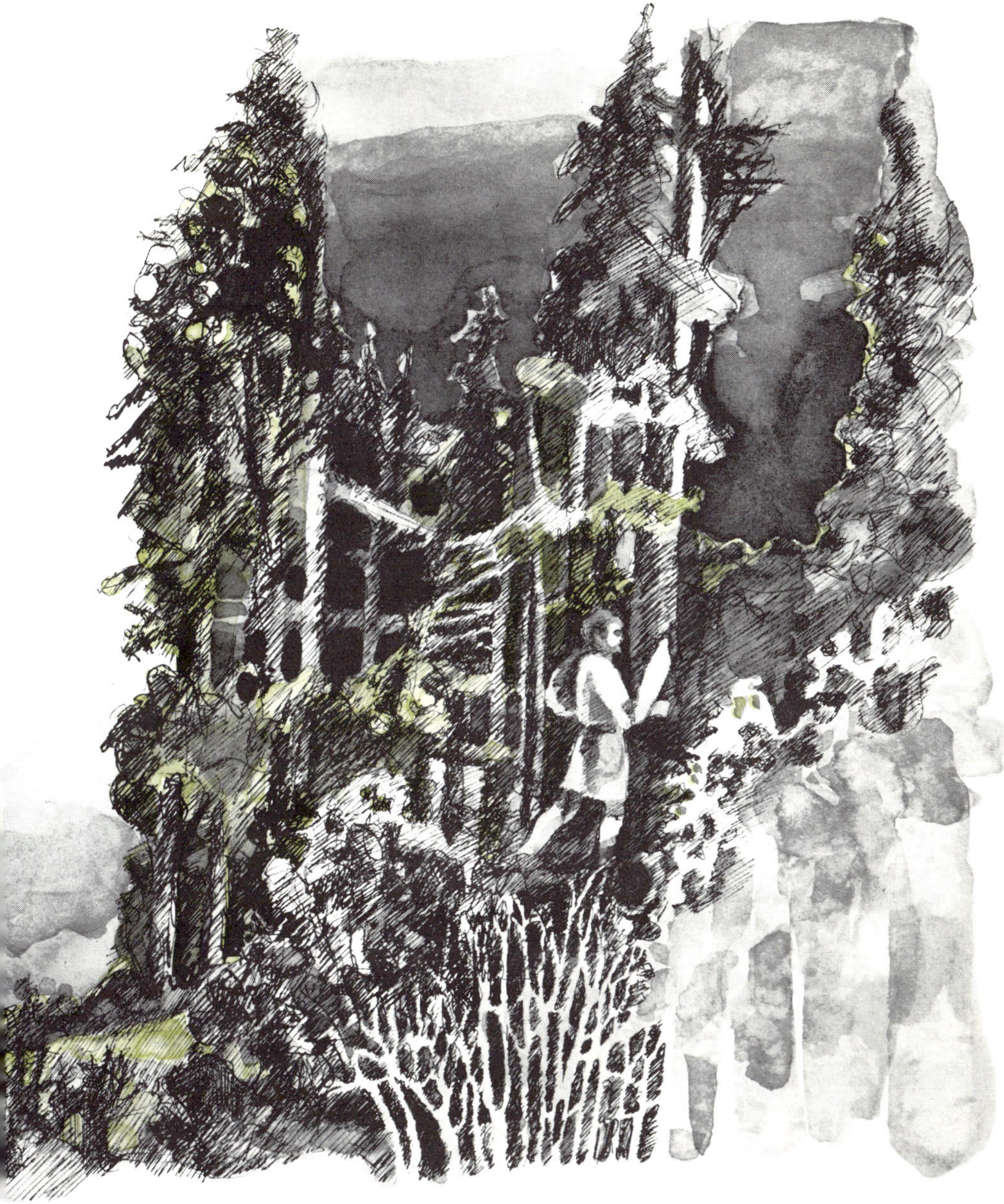

PHILIP WALKED ALL THROUGH SEPTEMBER AND OCTOBER. HIS FEET GREW HARD, HIS ANKLES STRONG; HIS SKIN was weathered and brown and his hair shaggy. The weather did not grow colder and he wondered if he had left not only his kingdom behind but winter too.

The falcon hunted well and Philip was never without something to eat. Sometimes he begged for bread at a castle gate. Sometimes he was given fruit by peasants. He walked through towns where hundreds of people lived together and the streets were more cluttered and muddy than the floor of his castle in winter.

He walked through vast empty stretches of country where he did not find one human soul. He walked through great forests which grew dark long before evening fell. Once he saw, at the edge of a field, a stag, golden in the last rays of the sun.

Often he was lonely.

He learned to read the sky, to take cover

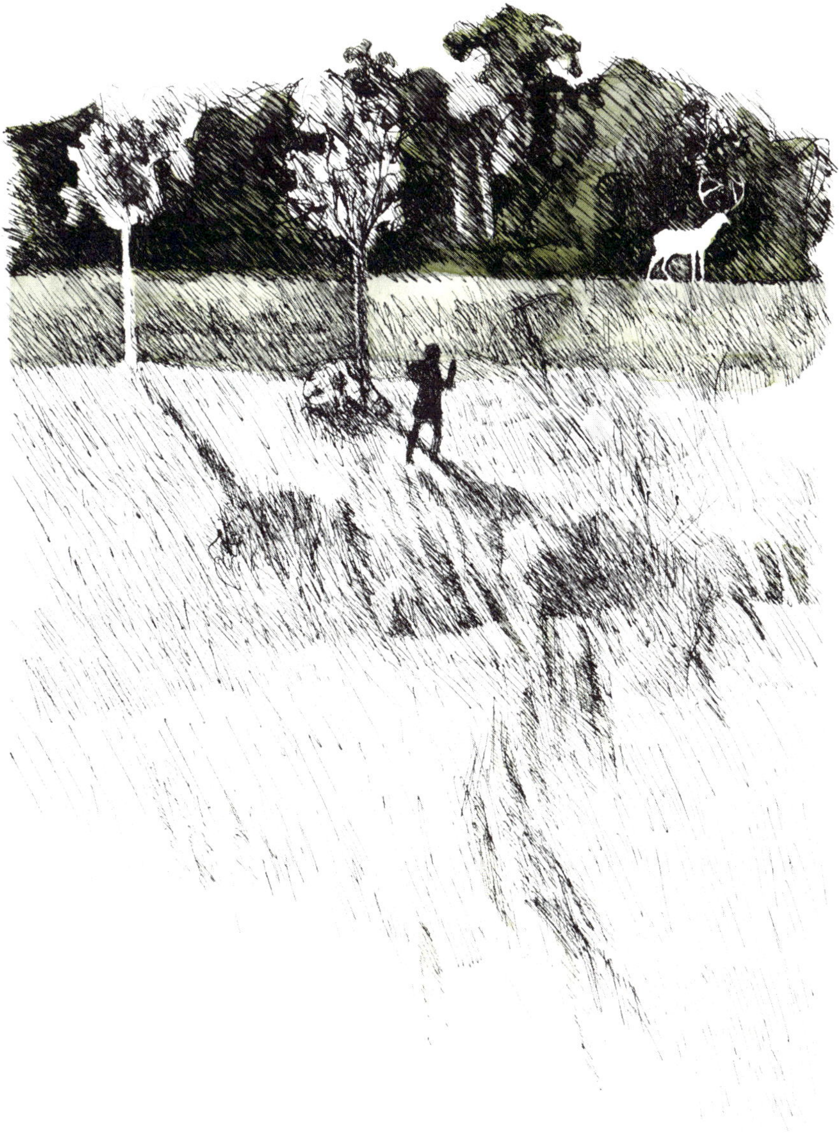

before the rain fell and the winds blew. He learned to make shelters from forest brush to keep himself warm when the nights were damp, and to pass through a sleeping village as silently as a ghost.

One night he fell asleep at the base of a small hill. Upon awakening the next morning, he climbed to its top and saw, stretched before him, green and blue, burnished and unmoving, the sea. Had he made a great circle then, and come back to the same shore? But he had noted the night before that the stars were not the same as those in the sky over his old kingdom. And the quality of the light was different, whiter, more clear, and the sun was hotter and strange trees grew in the sandy soil, trees with spiny leaves shaped like languid hands. It must be that he had traveled south.

 Then he looked to his right. There, a handsome castle rose from the yellow land. All around it clustered the huts of a large village. He set off toward the castle.

In a while, he met a shepherd half-asleep in a meadow surrounded by his sheep.

"Whose castle is that?" he asked.

The shepherd yawned. "Ah-h-h-h, King—ah-h-h-h—Renato's," he said sleepily.

"What sort is he?" asked Philip.

"Not bad for a king," replied the shepherd.

"Is it a large kingdom?"

"I suppose so," said the shepherd. "There are many knights and many holy brothers. What is that you are carrying on your arm?"

"My falcon," said Philip.

"And does she hunt well?"

"Very well," answered Philip.

"Go see the King, then. He is fond of falconers and musicians. Perhaps he will allow you to remain at his court."

That is exactly what happened.

The King, who was plump and amiable, was enchanted with the falcon. He had not had a falconer in his court for many years.

"We are not energetic," he said to Philip, who was standing before the throne, the falcon on his fist. "But we enjoy the energy of others. By any chance, do you sing or play an instrument?"

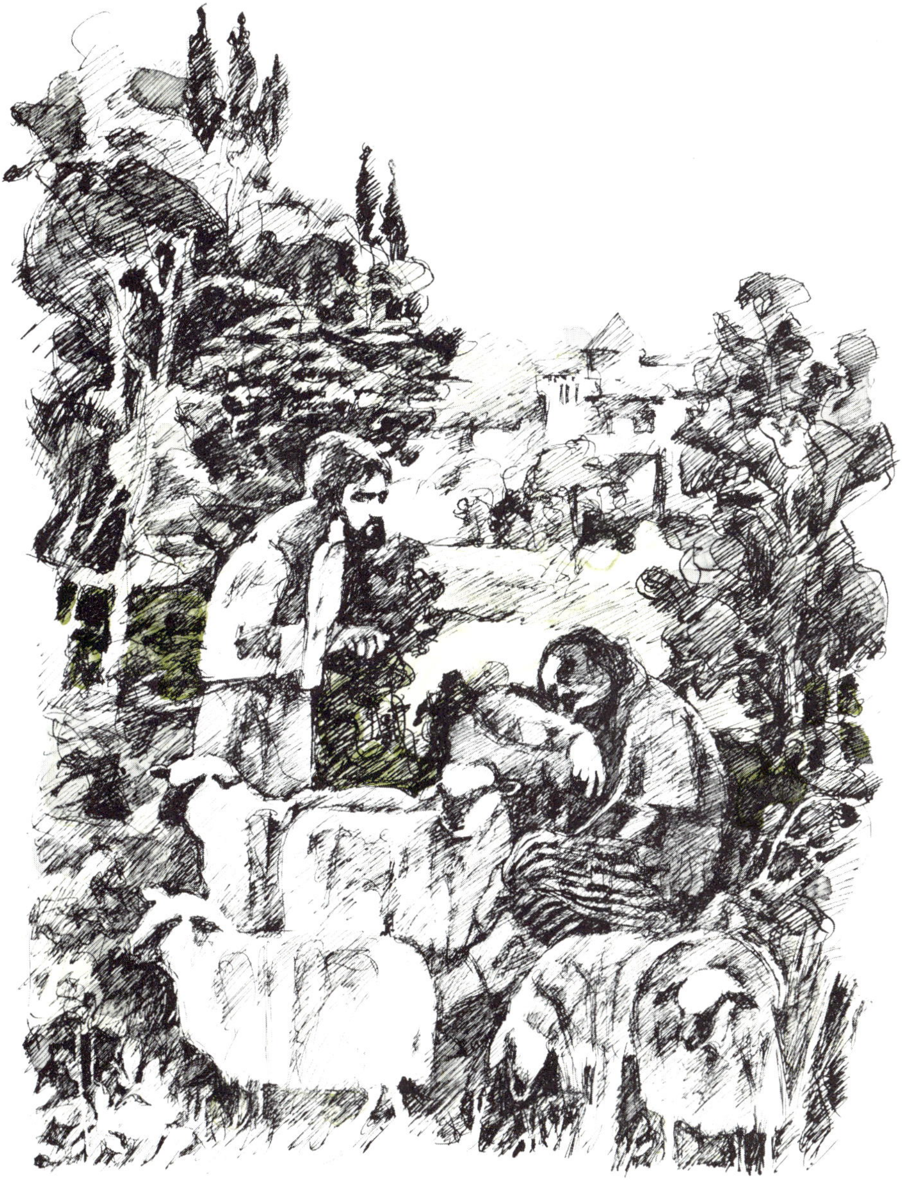

"I regret, My Lord, that I do not," Philip answered.

"Ah well..." the King sighed. "One can't have everything."

Philip was pleased to rest from his long journey at last. He was given a small chamber and he arranged it to suit an old dream. It was uncluttered and clean and full of light. King Renato's court interested him. It was so unlike his own. There were hundreds of people who came and went in the great hall, armorers and bakers, musicians and dancers, peers and prelates. As for the Queen, she was of a retiring nature and her face was kind.

Three years passed. The King grew fond of Philip who, as a man, was reserved, honest and tender-hearted although as a king he had been troubled and ineffectual. And when King Renato once remarked to him that he was fortunate to know nothing of the miseries of kings, Philip's former life seemed so far behind him that he agreed at once.

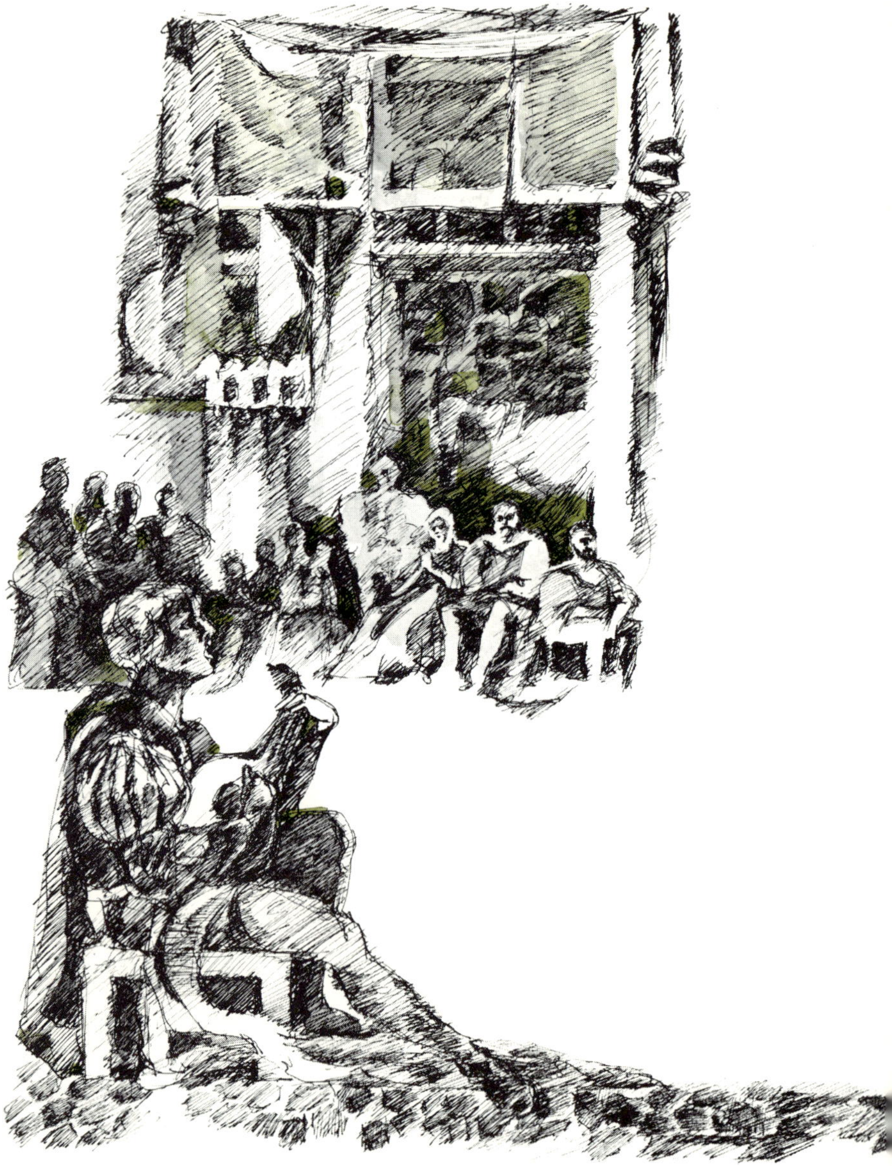

One night, a traveling musician came to entertain the court. Everyone gathered in the great hall to listen. The musician sat on a low bench in front of the throne. He plucked a string on his lute. Then he began to sing.

"Stop!" said King Renato. "I've heard that one too many times before."

The musician began a different song.

"No, no," exclaimed the King. "I know all about Childe Rolande. Try again."

The musician began once more, and this time the King did not interrupt him but settled back comfortably in his throne, a pleased smile on his face.

The musician sang of the king of a far country where snow fell most of the year. One summer, a falcon had come and lifted the king in her strong talons and borne him away and he was never seen again.

When Philip heard the musician's words above the sad, sweet sound of the lute strings, he hid his face in his hands. Behind their shelter, he was smiling. It is not often, he thought to himself, that a king can exchange his crown for a song.

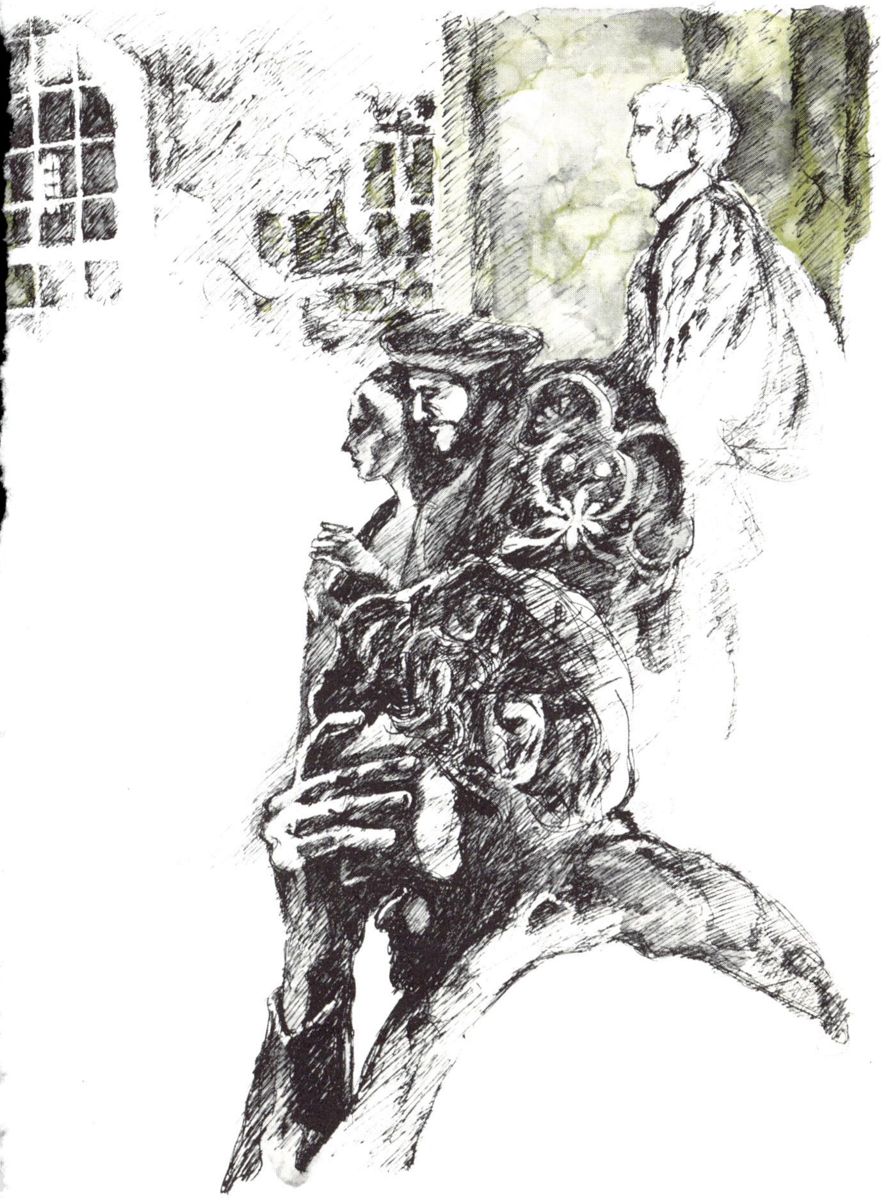

Books for young people by Paula Fox

MAURICE'S ROOM
A LIKELY PLACE
HOW MANY MILES TO BABYLON?
DEAR PROSPER
THE STONE-FACED BOY
HUNGRY FRED
THE KING'S FALCON